Real People

Martin Luther King Jr.

By Pamela Walker

Children's Press
A Division of Scholastic Inc.
New York / Toronto / London / Auckland / Sydney
Mexico City / New Delhi / Hong Kong
Danbury, Connecticut

Photo Credits: pp. 5, 7 © Bettman/Corbis; pp. 9, 11, cover © Flip Shulke/Corbis; pp.13, 21 © AP/Wide World Photos; p. 15 © Corbis; p. 17 © Underwood & Underwood/Corbis; p. 19 © AP/Wide World Photos/Horace Cort
Contributing Editors: Jeri Cipriano, Jennifer Silate
Book Design: Christopher Logan

Visit Children's Press on the Internet at:
http://publishing.grolier.com

Library of Congress Cataloging-in-Publication Data

Walker, Pam, 1958-
    Martin Luther King Jr. / by Pamela Walker.
    p. cm. — (Real people)
    Includes bibliographical references and index.
    ISBN 0-516-23436-6 (lib. bdg.) — ISBN 0-516-23590-7 (pbk.)
    1. King, Martin Luther, Jr., 1929-1968—Juvenile literature. 2. King, Martin Luther, Jr., 1929-1968—Pictorial works—Juvenile literature. 3. African Americans—Biography—Juvenile literature. 4. Civil rights workers—United States—Biography—Juvenile literature. 5. Baptists—United States—Clergy—Biography—Juvenile literature. 6. African Americans—Civil rights—History—20th century—Juvenile literature. [1. King, Martin Luther, Jr., 1929-1968. 2. Civil rights workers. 3. Clergy. 4. Civil rights movements—History. 5. African Americans—Biography.] I. Title.

E185.97.K5 W24 2001
323'.092—dc21
[B]
                                                                    00-065621

Contents

This is Martin Luther King Jr.

He helped many people.

5

Many people liked Martin Luther King Jr.

7

Martin Luther King Jr. liked to give **speeches**.

He became a **pastor** and gave speeches in churches.

9

Martin Luther King Jr. listened to people.

He did not like how **African-Americans** were treated.

Martin Luther King Jr. wanted everyone to be kind to each other.

He wanted all people to live in **peace**.

Many people liked his
speeches.

Many people wanted
peace, too.

In 1963, Martin Luther King Jr. led a peace **march** all the way to the White House in Washington, D.C.

Martin Luther King Jr. spoke of his dream for the United States.

He did not want fighting.

He wanted peace.

18

Martin Luther King Jr. was a great **leader**.

New Words

African-Americans (**af**-ruh-kuhn uh-**mer**-uh-kuhnz) Americans of African family origin

leader (**lee**-duhr) someone who shows the way

march (**march**) many people walking in a group

pastor (**pas**-tuhr) a church leader

peace (**pees**) a time of no war or fighting

speeches (**speech**-ehz) prepared talks

To Find Out More

Books
A Picture Book of Martin Luther King, Jr.
by David A. Adler
Holiday House

Free at Last! The Story of Martin Luther King, Jr.
by Angela Bull
Dorling Kindersley

Martin Luther King Day
by Linda Lowery
The Lerner Publishing Group

Web Sites
Martin Luther King, Jr. Day on the Net
http://www.holidays.net/mlk/
This site celebrates the life of Martin Luther King Jr. and his dream.

The Holiday Zone
http://www.geocities.com/athens/troy/9087/mlk/
This site offers games, arts and crafts, discussion topics, and language activities related to the observance of Martin Luther King Jr. Day.

Index

About the Author
Pamela Walker was born in Kentucky. When she grew up, she moved to New York and became a writer.

Reading Consultants
Kris Flynn, Coordinator, Small School District Literacy, The San Diego County Office of Education

Shelly Forys, Certified Reading Recovery Specialist, W.J. Zahnow Elementary School, Waterloo, IL

Sue McAdams, Certified Reading Recovery Specialist and Literary Consultant, Dallas, TX